ESCHATOLOGY
OF
AMERICA

FROM DESPAIR TO HOPE

Sarah Kim

THEOLOGY 3000
Chapter 64
ESCHATOLOGY OF AMERICA
FROM DESPAIR TO HOPE

"If religious books are not widely circulated among the masses in this country, I do not know what is going to become of us as a nation. If truth be not diffused, then error will be. If God and His Word are not known and received, the devil and his works will gain the ascendency. If the evangelical volume does not reach every hamlet, the pages of a corrupt and licentious literature will. If the power of the gospel is not felt throughout the length and breadth of this land, anarchy and misrule, degradation and misery, corruption and darkness will reign without mitigation or end."
Daniel Webster (1782-1852) – Former United States Secretary of State

"Keep this Book of the Law always on your lips; meditate on it day and night, so that you may be careful to do everything written in it.
Then you will be prosperous and successful."
(Joshua 1:8)

"Call on me in the day of trouble;
I will deliver you, and you will honor me."
(Psalms 50:15)

"Call on me in prayer and I will answer you.
I will show you great and mysterious things which you still do not know about."
(Jeremiah 33:3)

"Because he loves me," says the Lord,
"I will rescue him;
I will protect him, for he acknowledges my name.
He will call on me, and I will answer him;
I will be with him in trouble,
I will deliver him and honor him."
(Psalms 91:14-15)

The Lord Jesus Christ said:
"Until now you have asked nothing in My name.
Ask, and you will receive, that your joy may be full."(John 16:24)

FROM DESPAIR TO HOPE

Although shocked and saddened by the horrific tragedy that took place, the survival of Former President Donald Trump after a failed assassination attempt at an election rally in Butler, Pennsylvania, last Saturday has brought many Americans full of hope.

Hope, because through this event, they see that God still shows mercy and patience toward His America. It was He, who reached out His arm to perform a miracle to save Former President Trump. In this case, the former president's survival cannot be random. This is a miracle directly performed by God Himself.

We are pleased that Former President Trump was deeply aware of that. He said: 'I'm supposed to be dead.' "It was God alone who prevented the unthinkable from happening," "In this moment, it is more important than ever that we stand United, and show our True Character as Americans, remaining Strong and Determined, and not allowing Evil to Win..."

Former President Trump is more suitable for the Presidency of the United States today than he was seven years ago. He speaks more carefully and behaves more humbly, and especially after this failed assassination, he will certainly realize that he is just a very fragile instrument in God's hand.

During his previous four years as President, God used President Donald Trump and Former Vice President Mike Pence to bring about great things for America. Let us pray that over the next four years, God will use him and Vice President James David Vance, if elected, to bring America from the brink of decline to "Great Again."

Let us also pray that God will open the eyes of American politicians so that they will see clearly that if they want to be elected to serve America and the American people, they desperately need God's help. The demographics of the United States today are very different from twenty years ago. The Republicans are increasingly at a disadvantage, and only through God's direct intervention, God's miracle, and God's exceptional help can they win the election and rescue America from decline. So, anyone who wants to make America great again must pray to God with all their hearts, read, meditate, and obey His Word, the Bible. Let us pray that God will open the eyes of American politicians so that they will see that "We are not fighting against human beings but against the wicked spiritual forces in the heavenly world, the rulers, authorities, and cosmic powers of this dark age" (Ephesians 6:12). The war that America and the world are facing today is between Good and Evil, Light and Darkness, Truth and Falsehood. This is a war between the King of Light and the King of Darkness. We cannot succeed in this fighting by our own strength, our own wit, and our own wisdom. Instead, we must pray to the Lord Jesus Christ, the Almighty God, who is the Way (the Solution), the Truth, and the Life, who is also the Light, so that He may give us wisdom and power to win and perform the miracle of turning defeat into victory.

Especially, let us pray that all American Christians will take advantage of this grace period to repent profoundly and fervently so that Christianity will be revived, for all the sources of our national blessing come from the Lord Jesus Christ and His Word.

Despite the move from despair to hope, I have decided to retain a portion of the content of the "Eschatology of America, The Pain of America," written in early June and published on Amazon in early July. I believe these will still be the big challenges the Trump-Vance Administration will face in the coming time.

A Golden Opportunity!!!

1. This is an opportunity for Christians to express their love for God and their love for America by voting to choose people who love God to lead America.

"Providence has given our people the choice of their rulers, and it is the duty, as well as privilege and interest of a Christian nation to select and prefer Christians for their rulers."
William Penn (1644-1718) founder of the Province of Pennsylvania

"Bad politicians are sent to Washington by good people who don't vote."
Daniel Webster (1782-1852) – Former United States Secretary of State.

2. This is an opportunity not for the Church or the clergy to participate in the Government (because that is unconstitutional and a disaster, a curse for the Church and the clergy) but for Godly Christians to, if called, participate in politics and Government to save America from decline, make America a rich, powerful, compassionate Country, and be a Blessing to the world.

Many of our forefathers, thankfully, were Christians. America was founded on Biblical principles; our laws based on Scripture... The secret strength of a nation is found in the faith that abides in the hearts, homes and families...Christians need to be involved in who governs our nation and how its laws impact the future.
Billy Graham (1918-2018).

3. This is an opportunity for all of us to turn away from all formal religions and all claims to be Christians in name only (because religion and the title of Christian cannot save anyone) and to turn back to the Almighty and Living God of the Bible, the Creator and Sustainer of the Universe, the Savior and Judge of the world.

"Seek the LORD while He may be found;

Call on Him while He is near.

Let the wicked man forsake his own way and the unrighteous man his own thoughts; let him return to the LORD, that He may have compassion,

and to our God,

for He will freely pardon." (Isaiah 55:6-7)

4. This is an opportunity for all of us to repent of our sins and receive the Lord Jesus Christ as our Savior. We do that so that the precious Blood of Jesus Christ shed on the cross can forgive and wash our sins, purifying our whole soul, mind, and body to become as clear as crystals before God and the universe.

"If we say that we have no sin, we are deceiving ourselves and the truth is not in us. If we confess our sins, He is faithful and righteous, so that He will forgive us our sins and cleanse us from all unrighteousness." (1 John 1:8-9)

5. This is an opportunity for all of us to receive the Holy Spirit into our lives, so that He can transform us into new creations, and make us children of God, "who were born, not of blood, nor of the will of the flesh, nor of the will of man, but of God" (John 1:13).

"Therefore, if anyone is in Christ, he is a new creation; old things have passed away; behold, all things have become new." (2 Corinthians 5:17)

6. This is an opportunity for every true son and daughter of God to solemnly and sincerely dedicate their entire life to God so that He can make it a Source of blessing, that is, an effective

means of conveying His love, His salvation, and all His blessings to the world.

"I will make you into a great nation, and I will bless you; I will make your name great, and you will be a blessing. I will bless those who bless you, and whoever curses you I will curse; and all peoples on earth will be blessed through you." (Genesis 12:2-3)

7. This is also an opportunity for the Church of God in America to repent: Repent for abandoning faith in the Bible to indulge in secular and worldly views; repent for being greedy for Power and Money; repent for losing love for God and others; repent for being lazy and negligent in carrying out the Ultimate Great Commission of the Lord Jesus Christ.

"Then if my people who are called by my name will humble themselves and pray and seek my face and turn from their wicked ways, I will hear from heaven and will forgive their sins and restore their land." (2 Chronicles 7:14)

Ten Disasters of America

Many people believe that the United States will 'fall' in front of China before 2050, and American civilization is in decline unless something substantial happens on a national scale to change the situation and reverse the process.

In human history, there has never been any country or civilization that is glorious, beautiful, powerful, compassionate, and brings more benefits to humans than the United States and American civilization. The United States was once a dream for billions of people on Earth, but the United States and American civilization are now rapidly declining.

Many also believe the United States will 'fall' in front of China before 2050. However, that does not mean that China will win the United States, but because the United States made itself lose.

The United States will decline itself, and now it is in the process of making itself decline.

The United States and the American civilization are self-declining because the United States is suffering from at least ten massive disasters as below:

(1). The first disaster is that the US is led by people who are, in fact, atheists.

(2). The second disaster is that the US Government has been corrupted.

(3). The third disaster is the erosion of American patriotism.

(4). The fourth disaster was the boom of Socialism.

(5). The fifth disaster is the reverie about Democratic Socialism.

(6). The sixth disaster is corrupt and destructive education, which threatens America's future and is causing an increasing loss of motivation and purpose among America's youth.

(7). The seventh disaster is that America has overthrown the foundations that built it and made it prosperous and powerful.

(8). The eighth disaster is Saudi Arabia's gradual loss of sympathy.

(9). The ninth disaster is the growth of BRICS.

(10). The tenth disaster is that America's greatness, elegance, attractiveness, American democracy, and American civilization... are fading rapidly.

I. The first disaster

The first disaster is that America is now and will be led by atheistic ideology and will become more and more atheistic.

The US is now led by people who are, in fact, atheists.

For more than 30 years, due to the negative things in the Christian Church and the declining trend of Christianity, thanks to the overwhelming success of American education in the direction of atheism and anti-Christianity, America today is dominated by atheism and anti-Christian ideology.

The statistics on atheists and believers in America do not mean much because atheism is atheism in lifestyle. Many people who claim to have a religion, such as Christianity, or even many who belong to the clergy, are actually atheists in their thinking and their lifestyle.

Many young people, because they have not experienced the new birth, because they have not had a personal encounter with Christ, because they are dissatisfied with the church, have become atheists and anti-Christian.

Most of the other young people educated and led very effectively by the American Federation of Teachers-AFT and under the very successful influence of the American Civil Liberties Union-ACLU have become atheists.

These young atheists hate Christianity and are very dissatisfied with the society that was built and influenced by Christianity, the American society. They are looking to create a new America, a new American society, a new American culture in the direction of atheism and socialism or atheism and democratic socialism.

More than ten years ago, former President Barack Obama declared that America was a secular country. Today, in fact, America is a country led by atheist ideology.

These young atheists are now leading America together with the old atheists. They will be the central voter mass and the masters of the country and American society.

But what happens when atheists lead a country that was built on Biblical faith like America?

1. America was prosperous, strong, humane, and free because It was founded on the Bible. Atheists who rule with beliefs and practices that are entirely contrary to the Bible and are declared foolish by the Bible, will undoubtedly cause America to become brutal, miserable, and decline quickly as the Soviet Union did in the last century.

The fool [a] says in his heart,
"There is no God."
They are corrupt, their deeds are vile;
there is no one who does good.

The Lord looks down from heaven
 on all mankind
to see if there are any who understand,
any who seek God.

All have turned away, all have become corrupt;
there is no one who does good,
not even one.

Do all these evildoers know nothing?

They devour my people as though eating bread;
they never call on the Lord. (Psalm 14:1-4).

And:

The fool has said in his heart,
"There is no God."
They are corrupt, and have done abominable
iniquity;
There is none who does good.

God looks down from heaven upon the children of
men,
To see if there are any who understand, who seek
God.

Every one of them has turned aside;
They have together become corrupt;
There is none who does good,
No, not one.

Have the workers of iniquity no knowledge,
Who eat up my people as they eat bread,
And do not call upon God? (Psalm 53:1-4)

Footnotes:
[a] 1 The Hebrew words rendered fool in Psalms denote one who is morally deficient.

2. Because those who do not believe that God exists will lack the ability to do good. The Bible says:

They are corrupt, their deeds are vile;
 there is no one who does good. (Psalm 14:1)

They are corrupt, and have done abominable iniquity;
There is none who does good. (Psalm 51:1)

But why is it that if one does not believe in the existence of God, one will lack the ability to do good?

I would say that there are at least four reasons:

(1). The sinful nature of man makes him powerless against sin:

The Bible teaches that man, whoever he is, wherever he is, and whatever time he lives in, unless he is regenerated and indwelt by God within and helped without, is utterly helpless before the power of sin, carried away by sin like the wind:

For all of us have become like one who is unclean,

And all our righteous deeds are like a filthy garment;

And all of us wither like a leaf,

And our wrongdoings, like the wind, take us away. There is no one who calls on Your name,

Who stirs himself to take hold of You; For You have hidden Your face from us

And have surrendered us to the power of our wrongdoings... [Isaiah 64:6-7]

I do not understand what I do. For what I want to do I do not do, but what I hate I do. And if I do what I do not want to do, I agree that the law is good. As it is, it is no longer I myself who do it, but it is sin living in me. For I know that good itself does not dwell in me, that is, in my sinful nature. c For I have the desire to do what is good, but I cannot carry it out. For I do not do the good I want to do, but the evil I do not want to do—this I keep on doing. Now if I do what I do not want to do, it is no longer I who do it, but it is sin living in me that does it. [Romans 7:15-21]

(2). Not believing in the existence of God and in the afterlife, people do not have an

ultimate law to live by and are no longer forbidden from anything.

Although many people in society believe that there is no God, they are not atheists. Although they say so with their mouths or even think so in their minds, deep down, they still vaguely feel that there is someone present in the world, so they still walk according to the law of conscience (good heart). Still, to a certain extent, when they completely deny the existence of God and His power over life, there is nothing that can forbid them.

In an important speech in 1946, Jean-Paul Sartre said:

"One day, Dostoevsky* wrote: **"If God did not exist, everything would be permitted; and that was the starting point of Existentialism."**

Existentialism was built and started with the idea of atheism: God did not exist, and therefore, everything would be permitted.

In the 1960s, when Existentialism peaked in France and Western Europe, there was an explosion of a movement of fast living, "absolute" freedom, and extremely irresponsible indulgence. Tens of millions of young people, especially students, shook the whole of France with a new way of life under the slogan: "All prohibitions are strictly forbidden!" (Il est interdit d'interdire)... and as a result it drove French society crazy for several years, until the movement had to die out because they themselves felt that they had utterly lost their freedom, were chained to sin, that everyone could not stand them, and they themselves could not stand themselves.

*Fyodor Dostoyevsky (1821-1881), the most excellent writer of Russia, 1864 wrote "Notes from Underground," which is considered a masterpiece and prophecy of Existentialism, but later returned to Orthodoxy and had a conservative religious stance.

(3). Not believing in the existence of God, that is, not believing in a providential, protective Being, makes people always live in insecurity and fear, and must always doubt, defend, and defend themselves against everyone and every enemy, like an animal in the wild:

This doubt and self-defense caused Stalin, during his years in power, to kill almost the entire Central Committee of the Party through many large and small purges. In particular, through many fabricated cases, he quickly executed most of the first leaders of the Russian Communist Party and all those whom he suspected of wanting or having the ability to replace him while he was still alive.

In his personal life, Stalin also displayed unusual insecurity and defense. He had twenty different sleeping quarters and twenty cars to travel in each night, and he decided at the last minute which car to take and which house to sleep in so that no one would know in advance. He also eliminated some of his close associates who served him in private areas to prevent betrayal or to cover up clues about his secret private affairs.

Hitler was the same. Living in insecurity, in an atmosphere of constant suspicion, and using the tactic of "preemptive action" to defend himself, Hitler repeatedly carried out terrible repression against those he did not trust. Especially after the failed assassination attempt on July 20, 1944, Hitler had the Gestapo execute or eliminate nearly 7,000 suspected military officers.

(4). Not believing in the existence of God and not believing in the afterlife judgment makes people commit evil acts without fear of punishment.

1. Example 1: During World War II, Hitler and the leaders of the German National Socialist Party waged a brutal war that killed nearly tens of millions of people and also killed at least 6,000,000 Jews and millions of victims of other ethnic groups in ethnic cleansing campaigns. But why were they so cruel?

There are two reasons:

(a). The first is because their leaders, especially Hitler, the Führer, and Himmler, the Head of the SS, were people who denied the existence of God and fanatically believed in Darwin's theory of evolution. They firmly believed in Darwin's prophecy about human evolution: *"Looking to the world at no very distant date, what an endless number of the lower races will have been eliminated by the higher civilized races throughout the world."* They believed that the German, British, and Northern European peoples, belonging to the Germanic race, the most elite part of the Aryan race, were a race that had evolved more highly than other races. And that the German race had a mission before human history to dominate in all aspects, from politics and economics to society and other peoples, and had the duty to purify society, as summarized quite specifically in Hitler's Mein Kampf.

So, in order to carry out that mission, on the one hand, they eliminated the Jews for fear of competition, and they eliminated the Slavs and the

Gypsies because they feared that the mixing of these two races might destroy the absolute purity of the German people.

On the one hand, they organized the selection of elite young men to reproduce for the nation with pure generations while at the same time secretly eliminating those with congenital disabilities and deformities from the German people, whom they believed were defective in the process of natural selection.

(b). Secondly, because they denied the existence of God, the Nazi leaders believed that death was the end, that there was nothing left. The ideal and purpose of life was this life: to find glory while alive and to receive praise from posterity after death. Those close to Hitler said that he often recited an ancient Viking poem, which he was very proud of:

"All things will pass away,
Nothing remains,
Except for the glory of the dead,
That will last forever."

With his belief in evolution and atheism, Hitler had little idea of sin and could not understand why murder was a great crime. With his belief in evolution and atheism, Hitler had little concept of sin and could not understand why murder was a great crime. The essential thing for every man was to be famous and to preserve his name. Therefore, if necessary, killing, as long as it brings glory to the German people and makes Germany known for thousands of years.

2. Example 2: Today, more than 80 years have passed, Russia and the Russians still feel extremely miserable about the fact that Stalin, during his 30 years in power from 1923 to 1953, killed nearly 20 million Soviet citizens, including millions of the country's elite.

For Stalin, killing hundreds of thousands of people was an effortless task. Once, after he ordered the execution of a top veteran leader of the Party as if to reassure the person carrying out the task, he said: "A hundred years from now, no one will know who he was. Just like today, no one knows the names of the people Ivan the Great killed?"

Stalin also said: "The death of one person is a tragedy, but the death of a million people is just a statistic."

But what could cause a person to reach such a level of cruelty when pushed by circumstances? Faith has no God, afterlife, or judgment.

II. The second disaster

The second disaster was that the US government was corrupted.

Lord Acton once said: "Power tends to corrupt, and absolute power corrupts absolutely." Although this saying is too old and too familiar, applying it to the current government today is still very accurate.

The current government has a talent for demagoguery. It does everything to make people forget or less angry about its failures in essential country issues.

Meanwhile, it is a great disaster for America because the US President and a sizable number of those standing with him in both houses of Congress and the States have been consumed by greed and the power enslaved. They do everything to gain power, and just for the sake of holding power, without caring about the damage, the danger to America, or America's future.

Here is some evidence that anyone can see:

1. They used American taxpayer dollars and borrowed money, in an extremely irresponsible manner, to bribe people they hoped would vote for them. In other words, they buy power for themselves with the American people's tax money and national debt, regardless of the country's future and the future of the next generations.

2. Buying the favor of some voters to win their votes by teaching about sex, transgender, and puberty blockers... ideas to children is another evil act stemming from the lust for power. This is an act that sins against God and an evildoing against humanity by those who are greedy for power and have been corrupted by power.

3. In particular, the prohibition on schools notifying parents if their child requests a change in gender identity is a crime that will destroy core family relationships, which in turn will undoubtedly destroy the very foundation of the family. The family has always been the cradle, the safe and happy home of a living creature, to raise a creature to grow. Advocating for children who are not yet mature enough to be allowed to make a decision in an election, but to be able to make their own decision like this, which is extremely important to their future, is truly an evil, unconscionable act.

God will punish a wicked nation, and when He does, the people will pay the price:

The Bible and history record that around the 8th century BC, the Kingdom of Israel was divided into two, the Northern Kingdom and the Southern Kingdom, because of King Solomon's sins.

The king of the Northern Kingdom was Jeroboam. He was a cunning man, and to maintain his people's loyalty, he used a political tactic: He deliberately created conditions for the people to commit sins.

He turned his government and the governments that followed him into evil governments.

Finally, after a while, the Northern Kingdom was invaded and destroyed by the Assyrian Empire. The people were killed and enslaved by the Assyrian army in an extraordinarily ferocious and tragic way.

III. The third disaster

The third disaster is the erosion of American patriotism.

Patriotism is a part of the Universal Morals and Natural Sentiments of humanity.

It is patriotism that makes soldiers sacrifice for their comrades and for their country.

It is patriotism that makes political leaders sacrifice for the people and the country.

But today the patriotism of Americans has been dramatically eroded.

There are at least three main reasons why American patriotism is being eroded in these days:

1. What hurts Americans' hearts the most today is how the country is run, making them not believe that the current ruling party is patriotic. The US government has implemented too many policies to bribe voters without caring about America's future prosperity or the interests and benefits of future generations. As mentioned above, they feel that those in power only love them, love power, love their seats, and love money, but they do not truly love America or Americans.

2. The US government, to please the atheists and the far left, has adopted policies that are very contrary to the conscience and faith of those with religious beliefs or universal conscience.

Three elements comprise a nation: the land, the people, and the government.

The government is one of those three elements. When a person loves his country, he also loves the government he elected and supported with tax money.

However, a person can only love his government when he sees that its policies and actions bring prosperity, strength, safety, and health to his country, community, and family in the present and the future.

America is a country built on the foundation of the Bible and Christian faith. Today, although many Americans are not Christians, they still have religious beliefs or at least live according to universal conscience and morality. They can hardly love an immoral government.

When a government is immoral, and its policies and practices are contrary to human conscience and universal morality, people with sound faith and conscience cannot love it, and patriotism is severely eroded.

3. American patriotism was significantly eroded after the Jan 06, 2024 incident.

The January 6, 2020, riot was a thoughtless act by people desperate for America's future. They are hopeless because they believe that election integrity, the foundation of American politics, has been lost, and will be lost forever. They think this is the last chance to save the American election and save America.

They acted hastily and unthinkingly, but there is an undeniable truth: They are people who really care about America's future and sincerely consider America their homeland.

What happened after that riot was painful: The spending of nearly $2 billion to turn the Capitol into a fortress and the merciless, relentless persecutions of those rioters reminded us of what had happened in Russia, what the Bolsheviks in Russia did to thousands of Russians, whom they called "enemies of the people," after the failed assassination of Lenine in 1918. The repression of those who are patriots and have made outstanding contributions to America...causes pain to those who love America. They feel like American mothers are taking their filial children to raise wolves... And their patriotism turned into pain and despair. They were desperate because they believed the America they loved and were proud of had begun to enter the twilight of its decline.

As for my husband and I, we were heartbroken to read about the death of Babbitt, an Air Force veteran, who was shot that day. Babbitt reminds me of our child. Twenty years ago, when our son, who was also in the US Air Force, was deployed to Iraq like Babbit, my husband and I were apprehensive. However, my husband and I said, "Our family owes America a lot. This is my opportunity to contribute to America". We love America very much. We believe Babbit is the same...

The erosion of American patriotism is dangerous. Dangerous both in wartime and in peacetime.

In wartime, for example, in wartime, how can soldiers fight and die for a country they no longer love heartily, especially how can they fight and die for things they consider wrong or sinful?

People can only die for the truth, not for the error, and for a good government, not for a bad one.

In peacetime, a government primarily filled with people who love power, positions, and money is susceptible to bribery or corruption.

Especially when America is faced with a master of bribery, love traps, and intrigue, that is China.

Less than five years ago, when a former French President passed away, the press reported that this President, who had already left the presidency, had received 5 million pounds from Saddam Hussein just to do a "small" thing. It was to make a statement protesting the US invasion of Iraq.

https://www.dailymail.co.uk/news/article-7516175/Saddam-Hussein-bribed-Jacques-Chirac-5m-bid-make-oppose-led-Iraq-war.html

The reason the former President has had a bad reputation is because Saddam Hussein was only an elementary school student when he became involved in bribery.

This incident certainly could not have happened with China because China had a Doctorate in Briberiology thousands of years ago.

There is a saying that people often attribute to John Rockefeller: "What cannot be bought with money can be bought with very much money."

This saying may not be Rockefeller's, but if he did say it, he must have learned it from the Chinese because the Chinese knew it and applied it skillfully and fluently thousands of years ago.

If $5 million can't buy patriotism, then $50 million can. With 50 million dollars, some ladies of American politicians may sweetly and softly advise their husbands to "reconsider" a proposal or a suggestion from the payer that their husbands have rejected.

IV. The fourth disaster

The fourth disaster is the boom of Socialism.

The COVID-19 pandemic happened suddenly, leaving the United States with many consequences and severe damages.

However, the most severe consequences and damage are still the consequences and political damages.

What are political damages?

In a very brief way, in the aspect of politics, Covid-19:

1. Has created among Americans a mindset of increasingly living depending on the government:

(1). Mindset: the government is the savior

(2). Mindset: the government is the feeder

(3). Mindset: the government is the leader in every aspect of life.

2. On the other hand, Covid-19 has also built and developed rapidly in the US government:

(1). A totalitarian ambition.

(2). A rise of passion for power.

(3). An expansion of bureaucratic system.

All three will set in motion a process that could prove extremely challenging to reverse, potentially leading the United States towards a socialist regime or a society with socialist characteristics.

Socialism is a political model that history has proven that when applied in any place, it will make that place fall into death, poverty, injustice, brutality, and corruption, with no exception.

How can we believe that America, the cradle of capitalism, the first republic in the world with three separations of powers, fair elections, a free press, and the leader of the Free World, the country that saved the world from Nazism and Communism, may become a Socialist country?

Of course, America will not become a Socialist country in a day, a month, or a year, but it is entirely possible in the next ten to fifteen years.

Why?

Because America has been fully prepared for society and politics with a socialist mentality, emotion, and ideology.

In other words, America is ripe for Socialism.

And that ripe is expressed by:

(1). There is dissatisfaction and anger about the division between rich and poor, and there are always complaints about the gap between rich and poor in American society. Left-wing media often tell people that half of society's wealth is currently in the hands of a tiny group of wealthy people, and the remaining half is divided equally among the rest of the world.

But the Left-wing media very rarely points out to the people that the capitalists, the industrialists, and the middle class are the cash cows; the hens lay golden eggs to feed society because the three go out to do business, to create jobs, and to buy products that society makes.

That means they work hard to make large amounts of money that they can't spend all of so that society can spend it. They work hard to make products that they can't use all of so that society can use them. They work hard to build houses that they cannot live in at all so that society can live in them; they work hard to make cars that they cannot drive them all so that society can drive; they work hard to buy beds that they cannot all lie on so that society can lie on them, they work hard to make bread and meat that they cannot eat it all so that society can eat. (Ecclesiastes 5:11).

(2). Left-wing politicians also try to inflame a hatred of the rich and capitalists in the American people. For example, while in China and Vietnam, the "Socialism" government often proudly boasts about the number of billionaires increasing every year, in the US, there are politicians like Mr. Sanders Bernie and his followers, for example, do not stop attacking the rich and claiming that America doesn't need billionaires.

(3). The current American education system is promoting atheistic, materialistic, anti-Christian values and promoting Socialism under the guise of science, making children grow up blind to the truth.

(4). Meanwhile, in about 5-15 years, people over the age of 70 today, those who have the opportunity to have knowledge or experience about Socialism will be too old or have passed away. A generation that lacks understanding of the truth will replace their parents and grandparents as masters of society. It is this generation that will change society according to their ignorance. (Of course, a few decades later, meaning 40-50 years from now, these people will understand socialism through an experience like their parents and grandparents and be disillusioned with socialism. However, a U-turn from socialism is not an easy or smooth route.

Besides, by that time, that is 30-40 years from now, after decades under the Socialist regime, America has become too weak or may even be divided into many countries due to civil war, such as has happened throughout human history.

Moreover, China had long replaced America in leading the world by that time.

Additional reading:

THE PROGRESS TOWARD SOCIALISM

1. Are there cycles?

Socialism, at its height called Communism, was thought to have ended forever at the end of the last century but is now booming again.

The irony is that while Eastern European countries abandoned Socialism, today, the standard of living of the whole population has increased dramatically. At the same time, some countries still embrace Socialism, like China and Vietnam; thanks to "capitalization", the standard of living and the panorama of social life have changed at a dizzying rate, and they are now two of the fastest-growing countries in the world; Now, in many capitalist countries, a lot of people are dreaming about Socialism.

Why did the former socialist nations abandon this "ism" and are now on the path of capitalist development, or as China and Vietnam, which still claim to be consistent with socialism, are at the same time living and making rich capitalistically, while in the West, in some European and some

American countries, including the United States, Socialism appears to be gaining momentum?

Because as long as this world is still a world of lost, humanity is still an orphaned humanity; people do not know God, their Creator, people do not know Jesus Christ, the way to the Father; people do not know the purpose of life, and life is still suffering a lot; Socialism will still attract people, especially people who have never experienced living through Socialism.

Actually, the slogan and goal of the 20th Century Socialist, which fascinated billions of people like:

"Chacun travaillera selon ses forces et recevra selon ses besoins".
各盡所能、各取所需
(From each according to his ability, to each according to his needs!)

Today, one might not believe in it anymore. However, the goals and slogans for equality and equal distribution of assets and opportunities inherent since the French Revolution still attract many people.

2. How do they reach those goals?

The natural question for all of us is, where are the people, and where is the money to accomplish those goals?

(1) Where are the people?

Of course, since the socialist government has taken over all responsibilities, it must recruit more government workers, that is, "people's servants," to have enough people to take care of all the people's needs.

Recruiting more will create an increasingly hypertrophic bureaucracy. This is the characteristic of the socialist state: a large army of servants. In capitalist countries, on average, 20 people are needed to raise a civil servant. Meanwhile, in socialist countries, on average, every 7-10 people have to raise a "servant of the people" to "serve" them.

Expanding into all areas of society and becoming a totalitarian state, the government's power will increase to the maximum, and the ranks of high-class people's servants will become a ruling class, reigning royal-like that Milovan Djilas, the leader and philosopher of the World Communist Party, called it "The New Class."

This class became more and more powerful. The reason is that the socialist government gradually became the board of directors of an orphanage or a state-level hospice. People must live depending on the government, which is the goal and essence of Socialism. Everyone must cling to the government to live, despite living in the standards of the hospice. With full use of national resources, human resources, and very loyal forces (court, police, and military...) in hand, the government becomes an invincible force that cannot be overthrown.

Moreover, socialist governments always have a party member force with millions of absolutely loyal gunmen, along with their families, who are nourished and favored by the regime. Here's what Stalin did: During the purges of the 1930s, he ordered the collection of all farm produce to be taken away, saying that it would be evenly distributed throughout the country. He then created a fake food shortage so that millions of people, whose loyalty he doubted, could starve, and at the same time, he fed their cadres and families well. After being treated well and full of food, the officials were extremely grateful and loyal to their leader.

Former President Ronald Reagan, a wise and compassionate leader, was acutely aware of the pernicious effects of Socialism. He understood that the lazy and corrupt bureaucracy of a socialist government would "consume" a massive part of the nation's wealth and impoverish the country. He also foresaw that implementing socialist-style policies in America could lead it down a path of poverty and misery, prompting him to question the potential state of the country under such circumstances. Upon assuming the presidency, he delivered a crucial speech highlighting the government's burden on the people, and throughout his two terms, he tirelessly worked to alleviate this burden.

He once said: *"The scariest word in English is 'I'm a government man and I'll help you"*

(2) Where is the money? Raise taxes, borrow debt, and sell national resources.

Raise taxes: Whose tax increase? Of course, even if you want to, you can't tax people with low incomes and those who have to make a living using government subsidies simply because they have no money. Meanwhile, people with low incomes in a socialist society are getting increasingly crowded.

So, whether you like or dislike it, you must also raise taxes on the rich, businesses, and the capital class. But raising taxes on these classes would be a fatal blow to the backbone of the national economy.

Because without money, it is impossible to invest and reinvest. Loss of capital, plus draconian laws that left-leaning governments bind employers, the only action that the business owners have to take is to raise the price of finished products. However, when the price of finished products increases, the manufactured products lose competitiveness and cannot be sold. Enterprises doing business at a loss must go bankrupt or flee abroad. The unemployment army will increase day by day. The number of people the Government has to feed will also increase at the same speed. This vicious cycle will never end. The whole country will begin to go into poverty.

The more socialist society advances, the lower the people's living standards and the services businesses provide are also increasingly degraded.

All people who have had experience living with socialism have the same testimony: Goods produced in socialist countries are always and forever the poorest quality goods in the world, And the "servants of the people" in socialist countries are always and forever the most bureaucratic servants, most lazy servants, and most corrupt servants in the world.

Borrowing debts and selling national resources: Without the money to feed the burgeoning public bureaucracy and the growing army of national beggars, it is inevitable to borrow and sell national resources.

Tax increases, borrowing, currency inflation, skyrocketing prices, selling off national resources, and growing hunger are what is happening in Venezuela, as in the former socialist countries.

The preceding makes the following statements about socialism completely accurate:

"The problem with socialism is that you eventually run out of other people's money."
- Margaret Thatcher, Prime Minister of the United Kingdom (in office 1979-1990)

"If you put the federal government in charge of the Sahara Desert, in 5 years there'd be a shortage of sand."
- Milton Friedman, Nobel Memorial Prize in Economic Sciences

V. The fifth disaster

The fifth disaster is the Reverie of Democratic Socialism:

Some other American intellectuals have read history and know what Socialism has done to the people of those countries. Therefore, they no longer dare to think about Socialism for America.

But they are still tempted by a Nordic-style "Democratic Society."

We must admit that it is very attractive. But a Nordic-style "Democratic Society" is impossible in the United States because:

1. Scandinavian society is a small, easy-to-govern society. The population of Northern Europe in each country is only about 5 million. Only Sweden has about 10 million. In short, each country's population is equal to that of a large American city. The combined population of Northern Europe is about 28 million, less than 10% of the US population.

2. Nordic society is a long-standing Protestant society. The gap between rich and poor is low. The general knowledge of the people is very high. (Norway has the world's highest rate of university degrees.) Nordic society's level of kindness and honesty is also the highest globally.

3. The number of people needing social assistance across Northern European society is meager. While in the United States, the welfare budget is so high that it exceeds the country's ability to pay. According to predictions, this year, 2024, the US welfare budget will be more than 1,100 billion dollars.

4. Social evils in Northern Europe are also very low. The burden of court fees, imprisonment, and prisoner detention costs is also very light. In Northern European countries, for every 100,000 people, there are 72 people in prison. Meanwhile, in the US, for every 100,000 people, 700 people are in jail. This means the ratio of prisoners to the US population is ten times higher. Therefore, the burden of arrests, court fees, prison costs, and the cost of incarcerating prisoners is also ten times higher.

In particular, apprehending American suspects is hard work, a dilemma, and a painful societal problem.

5. Northern European culture is Protestant culture. The population is relatively purebred. Social consensus is at a very high level. The humanitarian spirit of volunteering to share, following the model of the Early Christian Church, has become a part of nature and culture. Meanwhile, America is a multi-racial, multi-cultural, multi-religious country, and there are fierce political struggles. That means Nordic Society is a society that shares because of love. Meanwhile, today's American society has gradually moved toward a society that fights for their rights because they don't love each other as much as in Sweden.

So, Nordic-style "Social Democracy" is just an illusion. If you start with Swedish-style "Social Democracy," you will end up with Venezuelan-style socialism.

*"Swedish-style Social Democracy" is not Socialism, but just a form of Love Capitalism. In these Nordic countries, the Government does not even set a minimum wage for workers like in the US.

VI. The sixth disaster

The sixth disaster is corrupt and destructive education, which threatens America's future and is causing an increasing loss of motivation and purpose among America's youth.

Everyone knows that children today will be adults in a few decades and will be the masters of society.

But American schools today are teaching children and youths things that are contrary to the Bible and things that have the potential to destroy the foundations upon which America was built.

In the old days when Christianity was still strong in America, the motivation and purpose in the life of the American people or young people, most of whom were Christians, was quite clear whether they said it or not: "Purpose of each person's life is to glorify God and to be a source of blessing for the world". Or to put it another way, more specifically, the purpose of life is to serve God, to serve others, and to be a witness for Jesus Christ" to bring the people to Salvation.

This purpose is revealed throughout the Bible and is the content of the Bible (Matthew 22:37-39; Revelation 19:10). The church often teaches this purpose, either directly or indirectly. Therefore, it is deeply imprinted in the mind of every Christian and naturally and automatically drives all their actions.
But today, Christianity has been weakened in Western Europe and North America. If you ask young Americans about the purpose of life, most will not get a definitive or clear answer.

Even the short-term goal, which motivates them to work and move toward educational, career, and financial success, is not something they can easily achieve in American society. People who fail and are not successful often experience mental crises, either mild or severe. This makes them easy prey for addictions, from food addiction to deadly drugs and fentanyl. The number of mentally ill young people number people addicted to drugs... in America is currently very large and is increasing day by day, directly threatening the future of America.

Besides that, "Where there is no vision [no revelation of God and His word], the people are unrestrained" (Proverb 29:18); the weakening of Christianity coincides with the deterioration of morality, causing the crime rate in American society to increase rapidly. The money spent on security protection, arresting criminals, trying criminals, and imprisoning criminals, especially for the cost of correction centers, has become an enormous burden on the US national budget.

VII. The seventh disaster

The seventh disaster is that America has overthrown the foundations that built it and made it prosperous and powerful.

So, what were the causes that made America prosperous and powerful?

1. America's strength and prosperity can be attributed to its foundation in the Bible: The pioneers who braved the journey to this land of dense forests and deep snows in the 17th and 18th centuries were devout believers. They left Europe in search of a place where they could worship God in Spirit and Truth and live out the teachings of the Bible in their daily lives.

The pioneers were unwavering in their resolve to build their families, communities, societies, and future countries, America, on the bedrock of the Bible.

According to the history of the Puritans, the Pioneers who came to Northeastern America, later called New England, were exceptional godly people. Every day around 4 a.m., whether birds singing or snow falling outside, inside the house, everyone kneels on the hardwood floor, reverently reading the Bible. At night, after dinner, each family must gather to worship God. The rule of the Church at that time was that any family head who was not faithful in holding Family Worship during the week would not be allowed to attend the Lord's Supper on Sunday.

When schools opened, all schools, from kindergarten to college, were first and foremost to teach the Bible. That's why the first colleges in the United States, then still American colonies, were opened in the 1600s and 1700s, such as Harvard, Yale, and Princeton...all following the same criteria: "to train godly and talented pastors and government officials to serve God and care for His people." Hebrew and Latin slogans such as "אורים ותמים" (Urim and Thummim), "Lux et Veritas" (Light and Truth), "Christo et Ecclesiae " (For Christ and the Church) engraved on the massive and ancient arches of these schools had expressed those criteria.

God said very clearly: *"Keep this Book of the Law always on your lips; meditate on it day and night, so that you may be careful to do everything written in it. Then you will be prosperous and successful. Have I not commanded you? Be strong and courageous. Do not be afraid; do not be discouraged, for the Lord your God will be with you wherever you go."* [Joshua 1:8-9].

"Prosperous," "successful," "blessed,"... And it's all thanks to the Bible.

2. America is prosperous because of Capitalism:

Some people often think that Capitalism came from Europe, but in fact, it is not true.

Capitalism originated in Philadelphia, a poor city at the time compared to other cities and regions in Europe, and then spread to the New England region. It was Calvinist Theology that formed American Capitalism, and Capitalism that made America prosperous and strong.

*"The Protestant Ethic and the Spirit of Capitalism" by the leading jurist, political economist, historian, and sociologist of the 20th Century, Max Weber (1864-1920).

3. America is rich and powerful because She has mercy and good treatment for the People of Israel.

As the Bible reports, Israel is God's workmanship, God's miracle, and the clock of human history.

The event of Israel returning to reestablish its nation after nearly 2000 years of dispersing is a millennium miracle. A people scattered around the world for almost 2000 years is now returning to live on a land already inhabited by others, reusing Biblical Hebrew as their official language, which has been frozen for 2500 years. Isn't it a miracle?

I have a friend who is a history teacher in a high school. He considers himself an Atheist and greatly admires Karl Marx. More than 20 years ago, he accepted Jesus Christ as Savior and told me: "I had the opportunity to study the history of the Jewish people. I also read biological materials about cells, and I am convinced that there must be a Creator, and that person is currently taking care of this universe. So I started reading the Bible more than a year ago, and now I have decided to believe in God".

God gave the people of Israel to humanity to be a blessing for all humanity. In addition to providing the Bible and Jesus Christ to the world through the people of Israel, God also used the people of Israel to contribute significantly to human civilization.

....

Since Titus's Roman army attacked Judea, laid siege to Jerusalem, and massacred the Jews from 68 to 71 AD, the Israelites were already scattered, then scattered even more all over the world.

Most Jews fled to Europe, where they prospered and made the countries in which they lived prosperous. But Europe is also the place that has brutally persecuted them. From the Roman Empire of the Caesars to Hitler's Third Reich, over the past two thousand years, Europe has brutally persecuted Jews through deportations and purges by anti-Semitism.

Ultimately, the United States was merciful and kind to them.

And vice versa, they also enriched, created wealth, and civilized America.

So that the Word of God, which had been promised to their Fathers, would be fulfilled:

"I will make you into a great nation, and I will bless you;

I will make your name great, and you will be a blessing.

I will bless those who bless you, and whoever curses you I will curse; and all peoples on earth will be blessed through you." [Genesis 12:2-3]

"May those who curse you be cursed and those who bless you be blessed." [Genesis 27:29]

Indeed, America blessed them by welcoming them* with kindness, so God blessed America according to the faithfulness of His promise.

For hundreds of years, God has blessed America according to His faithful promise because America has been a nation that blesses the People of Israel by rescuing and welcoming them and wholeheartedly helping the young Nation of Israel.

On the other hand, God also even used the Jews living in America to enrich America.

*The total number of Jews in the United States is 6,000,000. The total number of Jews and half-Jews in the United States is about 13,000,000, more than the total number of Jews in Israel and all countries around the world combined.

VIII. The eighth disaster

The eighth disaster is the gradual loss of sympathy for Saudi Arabia.

Due to religious doctrinal differences with Iran, Saudi Arabia naturally leans toward the United States and the West. Saudi Arabia is a strategic ally of the United States.

This relationship reached its peak when, in 2017, US President Donald Trump and King Salman signed a treaty in which Saudi Arabia would buy US weapons in large quantities of more than $300 billion within the ten following year.

But today, it seems that the relationship between the two countries is becoming less and less warm and close.

The reason is simple. Anyone who has paid little attention to the related events of the past four years can see it.

Perhaps Saudi Arabia has realized that with the deep divisions and unwillingness to recognize each other's achievements between the Democratic and

Republican parties in the United States, being an ally with the United States is not safe. It is unsafe because it contains too much potential instability, which people often call political risk.

Saudi Arabia has recently become closer to China, which opposes the United States, and is looking for ways to replace it as the world's leader.

China buys much oil from Saudi Arabia. If one day, Saudi Arabia does not renew its agreement to accept only U.S. dollars for its oil and accept the Chinese Yuan or the BRICS monetary system, Petrodollars will undoubtedly be weakened, and America's influence around the world will also be weakened.

IX. The ninth disaster

The ninth disaster is the growth of BRICS.

The BRICS, whose key member countries are China, Russia, India, Bresil, South Africa, Saudi Arabia, and Egypt... is growing. BRICS currently has a total population of nearly half the world's population, and the total national product (GDP) of the entire bloc is now almost one and a half times that of the United States. The growth of the BRICS in the last two years is a significant challenge to America's position in the world politically and economically.

That challenge will become even more significant in 2024 as dozens of emerging countries continue to express their desire to join BRICS, which is trying to create a common currency to replace the US dollar.

If BRICS achieves its objectives, it will substantially damage America's current position in the global economy.

X. The tenth disaster

The tenth disaster is that America's greatness, elegance, and attractiveness, American democracy, and American civilization... are fading rapidly.

From shortly after the country's founding until the end of the 20th Century, America has always been the dream of all humanity.

East Asian peoples such as the Koreans and Vietnamese all imitated the Chinese that called the United States America the Beautiful Nation (in Chinese: 美國, In Korean: 미국, in Vietnamese: Mỹ Quốc).

In Chinese, the word 美 "," is both the first letter of the three words 美利堅 American" and means beautiful and good. America is a very beautiful country in the eyes of all nations and people, in all aspects, from material to spiritual.

But today, the beauty of America is fading quickly.

Even some beautiful things in America today have become ugly and ruined.

While still functional, the houses, streets, roads, and overall infrastructure of the United States today do not exude the same modernity, cleanliness, comfort, and safety as they once did. We remember a time when the United States was hailed as 'the most beautiful in the world,' a title that seems to be slipping from our grasp.

Notably, social morality, the foundation of American civilization, is seriously deteriorating.

The United States, the pioneer of three separate powers and free elections, has long been a shining example for nations worldwide. This historical significance, this beacon of democracy, is now at risk as the integrity of our institutions wanes.

Besides the corruption of the US Government, the US Media is not truthful. The US Media, the fourth power of the US, is protected by the US Constitution and enjoys maximum freedom; it seems to serve Media tycoons rather than sincerely serving the American people.

This is starkly evident in the way the media operates. Instead of fulfilling its duty to inform, it often resorts to selective reporting, choosing what to reveal or conceal, and manipulating images. Many news reports released by the media quickly make people feel they are propaganda articles to defend or attack someone rather than information that provides people with the pure truth.

Particularly, Left-wing Media driven by Atheism and Materialism has also been in decline for a long time and is harming America. People believe that in the coming days, Left-wing Media will defeat the US by destroying the fundamental values of morals, the values on which America was built.

Root and deep cause of the above disasters

All of the above ten disasters originate from one root, from one profound cause: America has abandoned and overthrown the very foundation on which it was built: the Bible, the Living and Eternal Word of God.

Over a history of more than two hundred years, three elements have made up a kind, strong, and prosperous America: Christianity, which is built on the Bible; the American Family, which is based on the foundation of Christianity; and Capitalism, which was born from the spirit of Protestantism.

Separation of Church and State, separating Government from religion, was the right decision. Still, the decision of the Founding Fathers of the United States to build America on the foundation of the Bible was an extremely wise decision.

It is thanks to this decision that there has ever been an America and an American civilization in this world —a nation and a civilization that is glorious, benevolent, powerful, and full of blessings.

So, the solution for America and American Civilization is also evident and simple:

The American people need to return to the God of the Bible:

"Then if my people who are called by my name will humble themselves and pray and seek my face and turn from their wicked ways, I will hear from heaven and will forgive their sins and restore their land." (2 Chronicles 7:14)

The President and the Government of the United States need to carefully read, meditate on, and practice the teachings of the Bible, the book on which they placed their hands in oath, to be filled with grace, wisdom, and success:

"Be strong and very courageous. Be careful to obey all the law my servant Moses gave you; do not turn from it to the right or to the left, that you may be successful wherever you go.

Keep this Book of the Law always on your lips; meditate on it day and night, so that you may be careful to do everything written in it. Then you will be prosperous and successful." (Joshua 1:7-8)

The Holy Scriptures, which are able to make you wise for salvation through faith in Christ Jesus. All Scripture is God-breathed and is useful for teaching, rebuking, correcting and training in righteousness, so that the servant of God may be thoroughly equipped for every good work.

The President and the United States Government need to pray to God for prosperity, power, and peace for America, and America will be a blessing to the world:

"Because he loves me," says the Lord,
"I will rescue him;
I will protect him, for he acknowledges my name.
He will call on me, and I will answer him;
I will be with him in trouble,
I will deliver him and honor him."
(Psalms 91:14-15)

"Until now you have asked nothing in My name. Ask, and you will receive, that your joy may be full."
(John 16:24)

Why Is the Bible So Powerful?

1. The Bible is formed, preserved, and widespread in a wonderful way

The first book of the Bible, Genesis, was written about 1,400 BC, and the last book, Revelation, was written about one hundred years after Christ was born. Overall, the Bible was formed in 1,500 years or fifteen centuries.

During that 1,500-year history, God used up to 40 people to write down His will and plan. These people, from kings to prisoners, from prophets to fishermen, from scholars to shepherds, lived in entirely different social and political settings. But whoever reads through the Bible from beginning to end will know that this book has only one author and one thought, that the author is God, and that the thought is the thought of the Almighty Creator.

For more than 3,500 years, the Bible has been attacked by many powerful adversaries in every way to destroy it. But the Bible has not been destroyed. In contrast, today, the Bible is widely available in more than 2,800 languages and dialects, and hundreds of millions of publications are released annually. Even today, the number of readers of the Bible is hundreds of times more than the number of famous secular books like Shakespeare's Hamlet, Lev Tolstoy's War and Peace, or Victor Hugo's Les Misérables.

2. The knowledge of the Bible transcends wonderfully

Although the Bible is given to reveal God's plan of salvation and program for the ages, not for scientific purposes, what The Bible teaches, including scientific knowledge, also came from an amazing super-superior wisdom.

For example, the story, the order, and the way in which God created the world are the story that Moses entirely wrote thanks to God's revelation to him because there was no one there to record the process that God performed so that they could tell Moses, or even Adam what had happened. Therefore, scientists today must be amazed at its wisdom and its accuracy.

Also, until less than a thousand years ago, Chinese people still believed that "heaven is round, the land is square," in Europe, it was thought that the Earth was a flat plane. The Bible declared 3,500 years ago that the Earth is a circular sphere, suspended in outer space:

"He spreads out the northern skies over empty space.
He suspends the earth over nothing.
He marks out the horizon on the face of the waters for a boundary between light and darkness."
(Job 26:7 and 10)

Exploring the Earth's interior is complex and even more challenging than exploring space. Today, thanks to scientific advances, humans can fly millions of kilometers into outer space; however, they cannot dig into the ground more than thirteen kilometers.

And it wasn't until 1970, the year after Neil Armstrong and Buzz Aldrin landed on the moon, that the new science using a particular triad (P wave) determined that the Earth is a fire block, heating up to more than 6,000°C. The center of the Earth, the innermost layer, is a solid iron ball about 2,500 kilometers in diameter, surrounded by a liquid iron shell. Yet, 3,500 years ago, the Bible taught people great things about the Land:

"The earth, from which food comes, is transformed below as by fire." (Job 28:5)

Even when prophesying that the great war will take place in Jerusalem, the Bible also seems to reveal some weapons invented and mentioned only recently.

"This is the plague with which the Lord will strike all the nations that fought against Jerusalem: Their flesh will rot while they are still standing on their feet, their eyes will rot in their sockets, and their tongues will rot in their mouths." (Zechariah 14:12)

Or when discussing the last day of our planet, the Word of God says,

"That day will bring about the destruction of the heavens by fire, and the elements will melt in the heat!" (2 Peter 3:12)

Please remember that the above words were spoken more than two thousand years ago when humanity only knew swords, knives, spears, shields, bows, arrows, and the like. You will see that the ideas and such understanding are super beyond!

3. The Bible's prophetic miraculous fulfillment

In the Bible, there are countless prophecies, and these prophecies can be divided into four main groups: (1) prophecy of human his- tory, peoples, and individuals mentioned in the Bible; (2) prophecy of Jesus Christ; (3) prophecy of the people chosen by God, called Israel; and (4) prophecy of the future world after Jesus Christ returned. Except for the prophecies about the future world after the second coming, which is still waiting to happen, all other prophecies of the Bible have been fulfilled precisely in every detail, are wondrous, and are entirely verifiable.

In particular, the fulfillment of the prophecies about the people and the nation of Israel can be easily seen even by those who do not believe in God because they are so obvious. Such an example is as follows:

"As the sun was setting, Abram fell into a deep sleep, and a thick and dreadful darkness came over him. Then the Lord said to him, "Know for certain that for four hundred years your descendants will be strangers in a country not their own and that they will be enslaved and mistreated there. But I will punish the nation they serve as slaves, and afterward, they will come out with great possessions. You, however, will go to your ancestors in peace and be buried at a good old age. In the fourth generation, your descendants will

come back here, for the sin of the Amorites has not yet reached its full measure." (Genesis 15:12-15)

This prophecy, addressed to Abraham (at that time, his name was Abram, an eighty-five-year-old man with no children), was fully fulfilled when the Israelites, Abraham's great-grandchildren, emigrated to Egypt because of starvation. They were enslaved people for four hundred years and then liberated from the land to form the nation of Israel and take possession of Canaan, where they built the famous Jerusalem temple.

The Israelites were in Canaan for nearly five hundred years. Other prophecies, such as in Jeremiah 25:8–11 and 29:10, said that because of their wickedness, they would be exiled to Babylon for seventy years and then forgiven and allowed to return.

These words were also fulfilled when Nebuchadnezzar, King of the Babylonian Empire, destroyed Jerusalem and the temple and exiled the Israelites to Babylon. When seventy years were over, he raised Cyrus, King of the Persian Empire, to forgive them and allow them to return to their land and rebuild the city and a new temple called the Second Temple. This temple existed for more than five hundred years until it was flattened by the

Romans, and the Israelites were once again dispersed and scattered around the world for nearly two thousand years. For almost two thousand years, the people of Israel were without countries, and the Land of Israel was non-Israel-populated.

Finally, seventy-five years ago, in 1948, also according to prophecy, as a millennium miracle, the Israelites returned, the State of Israel was restored, and the city of Jerusalem was rebuilt, becoming the hot spot of international politics seen today.

If you do not believe in God, please read the Bible. If you do not believe that the Bible is the Word of God, please read the wondrous history of the people of Israel to see the mighty hand of God that fulfills the prophecies!

4. The Bible, the Living and Powerful Word of God, has profoundly and marvelously changed individual lives and the fabric of societies and nations.

In the first three hundred years of Christianity, the young Church of Lord Jesus Christ was brutally persecuted by the Roman Empire. In response to this persecution, believers spread the Scriptures to their persecutors with unwavering courage and boundless love. Their actions ultimately transformed the Roman Empire into a Christian humanitarian empire, a testament to the power of Christian faith and Christian love.

A few centuries later, beginning in the fifth century, the Bible miraculously transformed the people called "Barbarians" when they invaded like a storm to the West. By the power of the Word of God, the Bible, working in the countries they invaded and conquered, they were transformed and these "Barbarians" became humane and peaceful people. They are the ancestors of Central European peoples like Germany, Austria, and Hungary—Christian countries today.

From the eighth and ninth centuries, Western Europe was raided and conquered by the Vikings. But again, these infamous fierce conquerors were also transformed. They accepted the Christian faith and mixed with the indigenous people to become the present-day Western nations like England, Ireland, Normandy, Belgium, and Switzerland. When the movement Back to the Bible started, they were pioneers in practicing the Scriptures and becoming very humane and civilized people until now.

This "Back to the Bible" movement quickly spread to their old homeland, the places where the Vikings were born. The story of this miraculous transformation was continued, and the Word of God again revealed its power. The entire Viking countries, Norway, Sweden, Denmark, and Finland, became famous as humanitarian civilization nations. Until recently, when Christian groups migrated to North America, they brought the Bible with them. It is the Bible that built the two nations of the United States and Canada, two countries that have joined other nations, believing and practicing the Bible like Australia, New Zealand, England, Germany, Holland, Switzerland, Sweden, Norway, and Denmark...full of love and generosity, as we can see today.

And most recently, people can also mention the "Miracle on the Han River." But what is the essence of the "Miracle on the Han River"? Nearly half of the Korean people have received the Gospel in the past sixty years, becoming eager and excited about their faith and sincere to read, believe, and practice the Bible. And the result is that, of course, these people, like other Bible-believing peoples, quickly and naturally became civilized, powerful, and blessed.

5. The Bible changes the mind and fate of each person in an amazing way

There are billions of people who have been transformed through reading, believing, and practicing the Bible. Without fear of error or exaggeration, it can be said that no one under heaven has ever sincerely accepted Jesus and sincerely read and practiced the Scriptures without receiving a breathtaking change, a dramatic change in both the inclination, disposition of the heart, and the conduct of daily life. The Bible refers to this experience of profound change as a spiritual rebirth—being born again, becoming a new person. The reborn person is mentioned in 2 Corinthians 5:17, "If anyone is in Christ, the new creation has come: The old has gone, the new is here."

The born-again man is not only newly created but also has a new life, a new future, and a new destiny. The one who was born again by God becomes a child of God. As a child of God, that person permanently ends his orphaned situation, no longer having to try to manage for himself in life. As a child of God, he receives the hand of his Father, the Almighty God, who holds, feeds, protects, and cares.

The reborn, the child of God, is also forgiven by God and cleansed of all his sins in the blood of the Savior Jesus. The born-again person inherits the "kingdom of God." Each person's identity is recorded in the "Book of Life" in heaven. The reborn person no longer fears hellish punishment because his future is glorious heaven.

But what makes a person reborn? The Bible says, "You have been born again, not of perishable seed, but of imperishable, through the living and enduring word of God" (1 Peter 1:23). "The living and enduring Word of God" is the Bible itself. So the question is reversed: Why is the Bible so powerful to change billions of people so spectacularly? The answer is that the Bible is the living and enduring Word of God.

Dear friends, because the Bible is God's living Word, let us read, meditate, and practice the Bible to be saved, transformed, blessed, and succeed as the following counsel of the Bible itself states:

"The Holy Scriptures, which are able to make you wise for salvation through faith in Christ Jesus. Keep this Book of the Law always on your lips; meditate on it day and night, so that you may be careful to do everything written in it. Then you will be prosperous and successful." (2 Timothy 3:15, Joshua 1:8)

Dear Friend,

God is our Father. He loves us with eternal love. His love is so strong that, even though we turned our backs on Him, He still loved us enough to send His Son, The Lord Jesus Christ, to earth to die on the cross to atone for us. He made a way and created a solution so we could return to Him and inherit Heaven.

Jesus said that he is the way, the truth, and the life and that no one can come to the Father except through Him. So, if at this time you feel your heart touched by the Father's love and you want to come to the Father, then you can offer Him a prayer with the following general idea or similar:

Dear God, my beloved Father,

I know that You created me out of Your infinite love. But I have shunned Your love in a thousand ways. Dear Father, I know that I am a sinner. My sins are great before you. I know that all my property, all my merits, and all my good deeds can never buy me even a minute in Heaven.

But The Bible teaches me that The Lord Jesus Christ came to the world to find me. He died for me on the cross, and His blood was shed to clean me from all sins.

Dear Father, right now, in this particular time, I put my trust in Your Word, the Bible, and step forward into Your saving arms. Please accept me in the name of Your beloved Son, the Lord Christ Jesus.

Dear Father, right now, in this particular time, I open my heart to invite the Lord Jesus Christ to come into my life and live in me forever. Please be my Lord and my Master for the rest of my life.

Dear Father, from this moment on, I pray that the Holy Spirit who dwells in me sanctifies me every day, every hour, by the Word of God, the Bible, so that I may become more and more like my Savior, Jesus Christ, in love, kindness, humility, holiness, and wisdom...

Dear Father, from this moment on, grant me a new life: a life of love, a life of service to You, a life spent serving others, so I can express my gratitude for the love and salvation You have given me.

Dear Father, please grant me to be full of grace in all things and all places, both in Your sight and in the sight of men. Please help me to be successful and prosperous in everything I do.

Dear Father, I ask You to write my name in the Book of Life in Heaven. One day, when I leave this world, Please take me to that blessed place so I can be with You forever.

I pray in the name of the Savior, Jesus Christ, Amen.

"Because he loves me," says the Lord,
"I will rescue him;
I will protect him, for he acknowledges my
name.
He will call on me, and I will answer him;
I will be with him in trouble,
I will deliver him and honor him."
(Psalms 91:14-15)

SARAH KIM

Sarahkimd2021@gmail.com

Made in United States
Troutdale, OR
10/03/2024

23398111R00046